OXFORD

UNIVERSITY PRESS

Great Clarendon Street, Oxford OX2 6DP
Oxford is a registered trade mark of Oxford University Press
in the UK and in certain other countries

Database right Oxford University Press (maker)

First published 2005 by Oxford University Press

British Library Cataloguing in Publication Data

Data available

ISBN 10: 0-19-911288-6

ISBN 13: 978-0-19-911288-3

1 3 5 7 9 10 8 6 4 2

Printed in Singapore

THE MAGIC ROUNDABOUT

PICTURE DICTIONARY

LEARN WITH THE MAGIC ROUNDABOUT

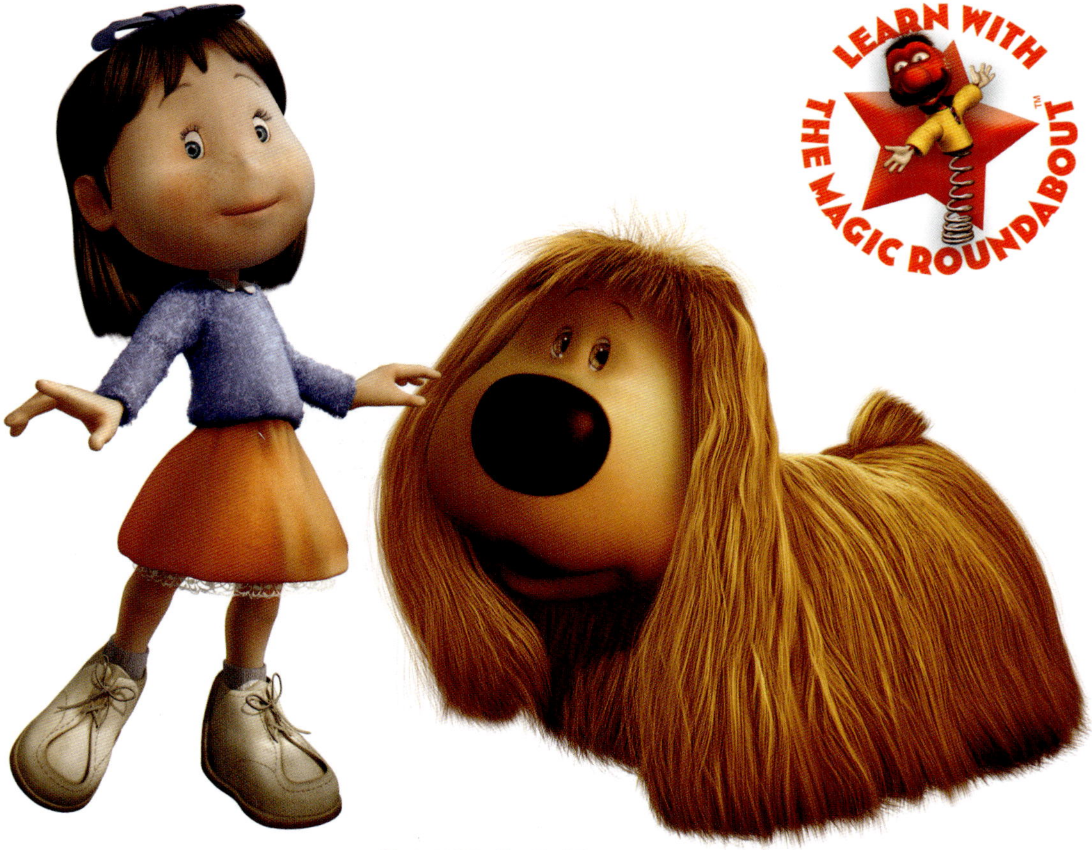

OXFORD

UNIVERSITY PRESS

Contents

Introduction

The 'Magic Roundabout Picture Dictionary' uses the characters and words from The Magic Roundabout to introduce children to the features of a dictionary. It contains over 300 words in alphabetical order. Each word has a simple example sentence illustrated by a colour picture. There is also a special section at the back of the book with words that children will find useful in their writing.

The words in the dictionary have been chosen to support and develop children's speaking, reading, and writing. Children will enjoy looking at the picture section and learning about colours, days of the week, months of the year, numbers and much, much more.

alphabet

capital letter

lower case letter

symbol for a verb

picture

fun phrases using
the letter of the
alphabet

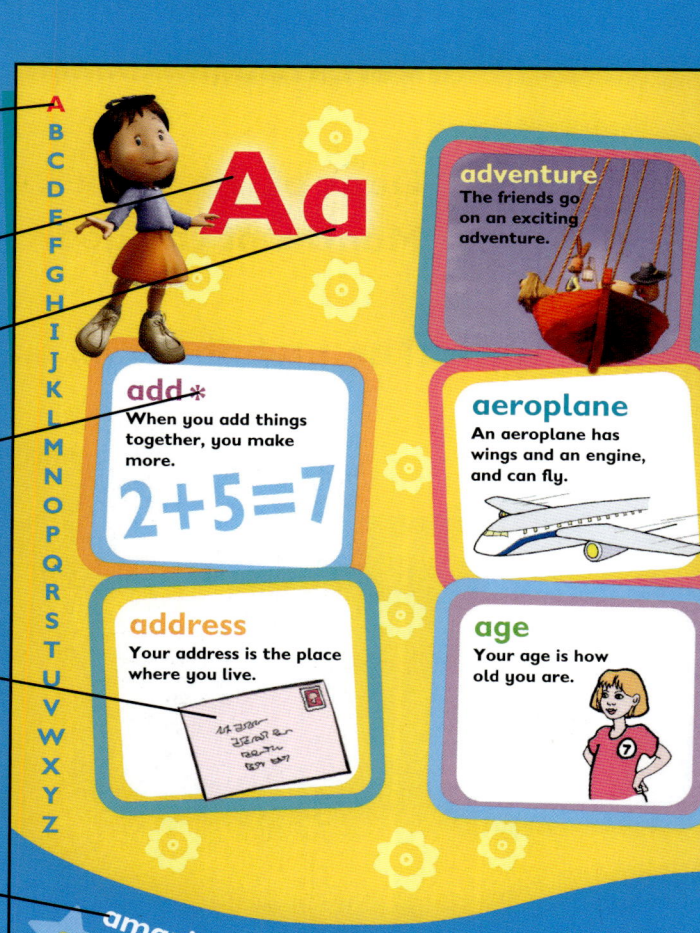

adventure
The friends go on an exciting adventure.

aeroplane
An aeroplane has wings and an engine, and can fly.

add *
When you add things together, you make more.

$$2+5=7$$

address
Your address is the place where you live.

age
Your age is how old you are.

amazing animals and abc

The 'Magic Roundabout Picture Dictionary' is an ideal introduction to dictionaries and other alphabetically ordered reference books. Using the appealing and familiar characters from the story, it teaches basic dictionary skills in an enjoyable way.

The A-Z pages will allow children to learn about the alphabet and alphabetical order; find a word using the initial letter and enjoy fun phrases using alliteration at the bottom of each spread.

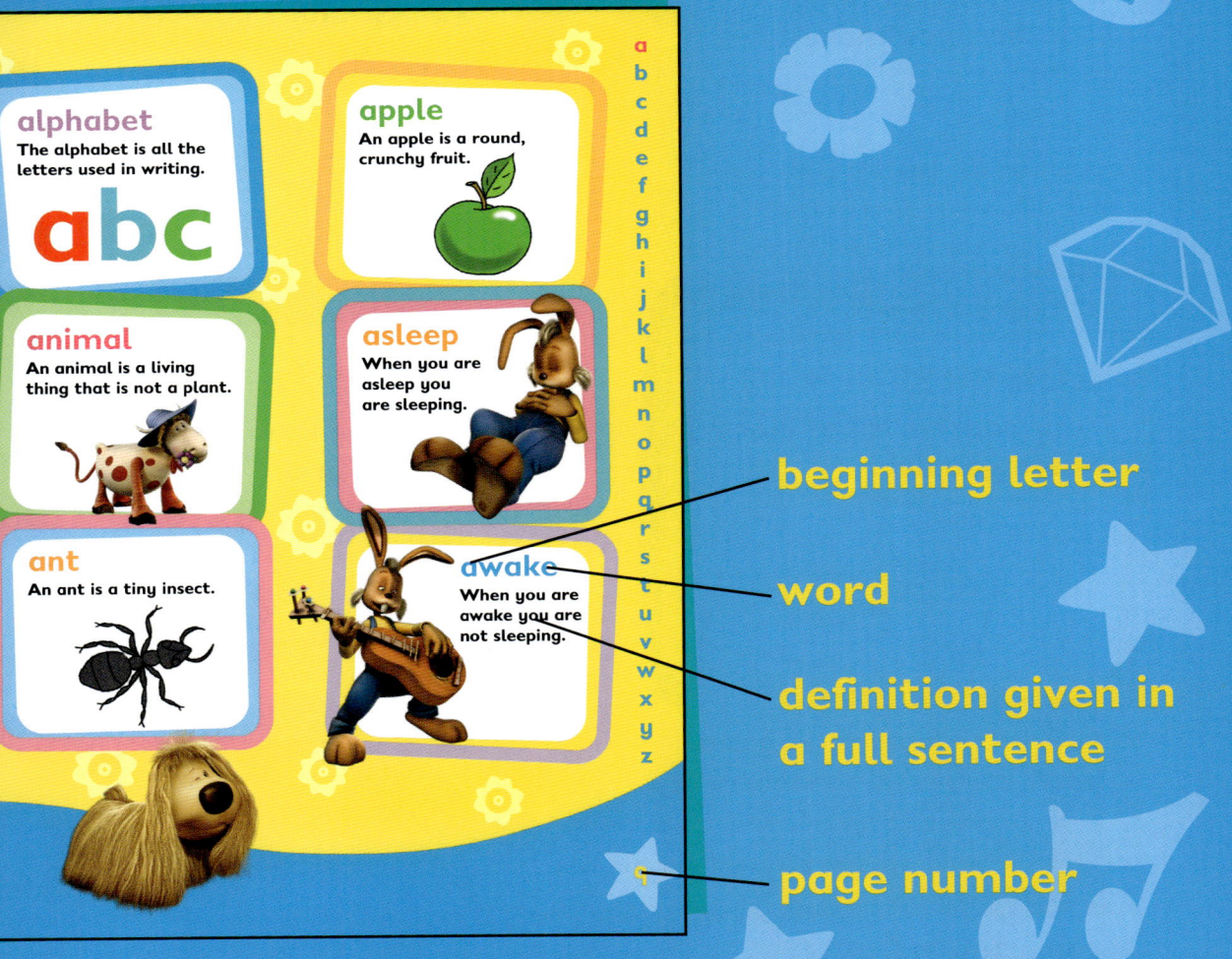

beginning letter

word

definition given in a full sentence

page number

Aa

adventure
The friends go on an exciting adventure.

add *
When you add things together, you make more.

$$2+5=7$$

aeroplane
An aeroplane has wings and an engine, and can fly.

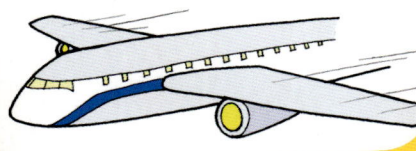

address
Your address is the place where you live.

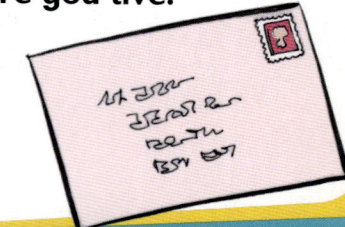

age
Your age is how old you are.

amazing animals and abc

alphabet

The alphabet is all the letters used in writing.

apple

An apple is a round, crunchy fruit.

animal

An animal is a living thing that is not a plant.

asleep

When you are asleep you are sleeping.

ant

An ant is a tiny insect.

awake

When you are awake you are not sleeping.

a b c d e f g h i j k l m n o p q r s t u v w x y z

Bb

ball

A ball is round. You can play games with it.

baby

A baby is a very young child.

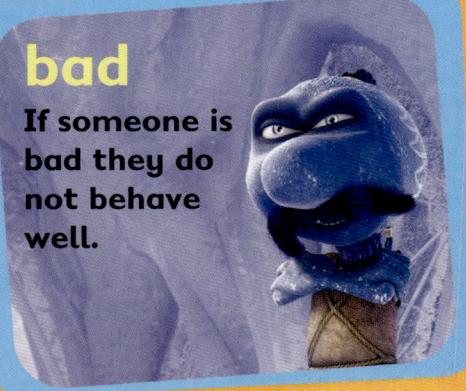

balloon

The friends use a balloon filled with hot air to float away from the volcano.

bad

If someone is bad they do not behave well.

bed

You sleep in a bed.

bashful Brian I can see

bird

A bird is an animal with wings, feathers, and a beak.

boy

A boy is a young male person.

book

A book has pages and a cover.

brave

When you are brave you are not afraid.

bounce *

Zebedee bounces off the ground on his spring.

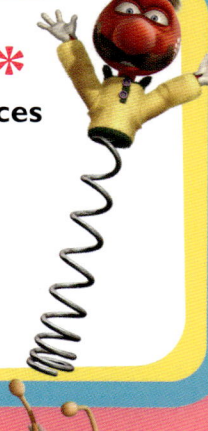

bridge

Train uses a bridge to cross over a deep valley.

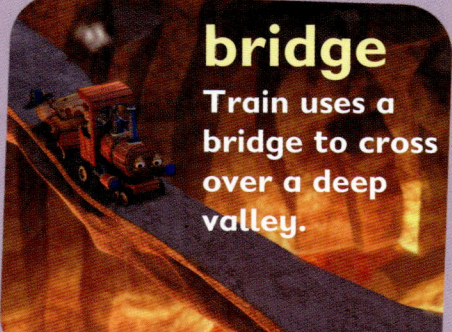

Cc

cat

A cat is a small furry animal.

cake
A cake is a sweet food.

child
A child is a young girl or boy. Florence is a child.

car
A car has wheels and an engine.

clock
A clock tells you the time.

clever cow just likes to chew

closed

When something is closed it is not open.

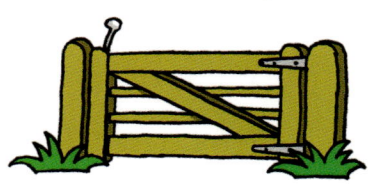

cow

A cow is a farm animal that gives milk. Ermintrude is a cow.

cold

Florence shivers in the cold inside the frozen Magic Roundabout.

cross

When you are cross you are angry.

computer

A computer is a machine that stores information.

cry *

When you cry tears fall from your eyes.

A B C D E F G H I J K L M N O P Q R S T U V W X Y Z

Dd

day
It is light during the day.

dance *
When you dance you move about to music.

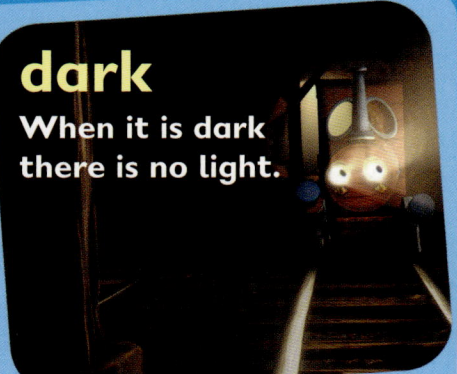

diamond
A diamond is a precious stone. The friends must find three diamonds.

dark
When it is dark there is no light.

dog
A dog is an animal you can keep as a pet. Dougal is a dog.

daring Dougal dashes around

door

You open a door to go into a room.

dress

Girls and women sometimes wear a dress.

draw *

You draw pictures with a pencil, pen or crayon.

drink *

When you drink a liquid you swallow it.

dream *

When you dream you see and hear things in your sleep.

duck

A duck is a bird that lives mostly on water.

a b c d e f g h i j k l m n o p q r s t u v w x y z

Ee

egg
An egg has a thin hard shell.

earth
You live on the planet Earth.

elephant
An elephant is a grey animal with a long nose called a trunk.

eat *
Dougal loves to eat sweet foods.

empty
If something is empty it has nothing in it.

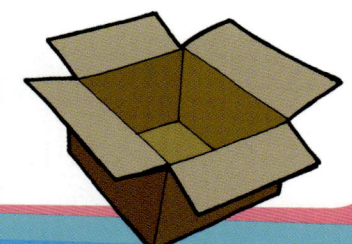

elegant Ermintrude would like some fun

end

The end is the last part of something.

evening

The evening is the time at the end of the day.

error

An error is a mistake.

$$2+2= \cancel{3}\ 4$$

evil

If someone is evil they are wicked. Zeebad is evil.

escape *

When you escape you get away.

exercise *

You need to exercise to keep fit.

Ff

find *

The friends look for the diamonds to find them.

fall *

When you fall you hit the ground quickly.

fire

A fire is something burning. It is hot and bright.

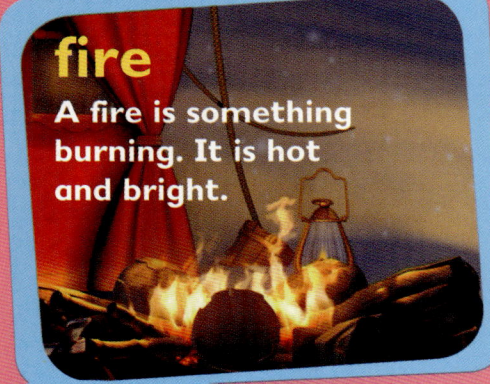

feather

Birds have feathers instead of fur or hair.

flower

A flower is part of a plant.

friendly Florence starts to run

food

Food is what you eat to grow.

fruit

You can eat fruit. Apples and oranges are fruit.

freeze *

When something freezes it becomes really cold, like ice.

full

When something is full it cannot contain any more.

friend

A friend is someone you like, and who likes you too. Florence and Dougal are friends.

fur

Fur is the soft hair that covers some animals.

A B C D E F G H I J K L M N O P Q R S T U V W X Y Z

Gg

giant

A giant is a very big person.

game

You play a game.

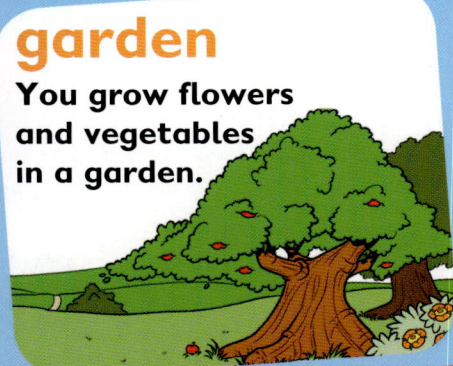

girl

A girl is a young female person. Florence is a girl.

garden

You grow flowers and vegetables in a garden.

glass

A window is made of glass.

go *
When something goes it moves.

greedy
If you are greedy you want to eat more food than you need.

good
Zebedee is a good wizard whose magic helps people.

grow *
Things get bigger when they grow.

grass
Grass is a green plant that grows in gardens and fields.

guitar
Dylan plays the strings of his guitar to make music.

Hh

hide ✳

When you hide you get into a place where you cannot be seen.

happy

When you are happy you feel good.

hill

A hill is a piece of high land.

hat

Ermintrude wears a hat on her head.

hole

A hole is a gap in something.

happy Brian with hat on head

holiday

A holiday is when you do not go to school or work.

hot

If something is hot it can burn you. Fire is hot.

horse

You can ride a horse.

house

You can live in a house.

hospital

You may go to a hospital if you are ill.

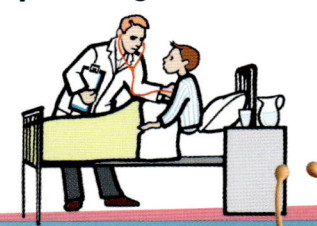

hungry

If you are hungry you want to eat. Dougal is often hungry.

Ii

ill

If you are ill you do not feel well.

ice

Zeebad lives in a freezing palace made of ice.

insect

An insect is a small animal with six legs.

igloo

An igloo is a house made of blocks of hard snow.

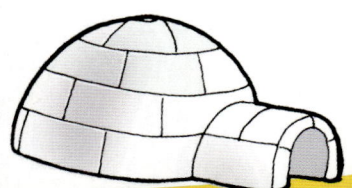

instrument

You use an instrument to make music.

ice and icicles are freezing cold

Jj

jug
You use a jug to pour a drink.

jam
You make jam with fruit and sugar.

jump *
When you jump, you go up into the air.

journey
The friends travel on a journey from one place to another.

jungle
A jungle is a forest in a hot country.

jumping joker, oh so bold

Kk

kick *

You kick a ball with your foot.

keep *

If you keep something you do not give it away.

kind

If someone is kind they are nice to you.

key

You use a key to open a lock.

king

A king is a man who rules a country.

keep-fit Dylan karate kicks

Ll

letter
You use letters to write words.

e g a

ladder
A ladder has rungs you can climb up and down.

light
When it is light you can see.

laugh *
You laugh if something is funny.

like *
If you like someone you think they are nice. Dougal likes Florence.

laugh at Zeebad's little tricks

little

If something is little it is not big.

lose *

If you lose something you cannot find it.

lock

A lock is opened with a key.

loud

Ermintrude's voice is loud when she sings.

look *

You use your eyes to look.

love *

When you love someone you like them very much.

Mm

map

The friends have a map to show them where the diamonds are.

magic

Magic makes impossible things happen.

march *

Soldier Sam marches in a straight line.

make *

You make something by putting things together.

mend

You mend something which is broken.

magic music makes a sound

money

You use money to buy things.

moose

A moose is a large furry animal with antlers.

monster

Monsters attack the friends in the temple.

mountain

A mountain is a high hill.

moon

You often see the moon in the sky at night.

mouse

A mouse is a small animal with a long tail.

Nn

night
It is dark during the night.

name
Your name is what people call you.

BRIAN DYLAN FLORENCE

no
You say no when you do not want something.

new
Something is new when you first get it.

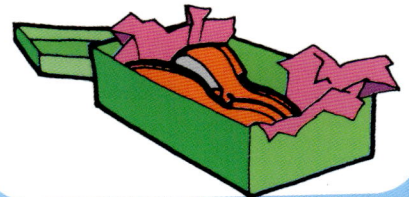

noise
A noise is a sound.

A B C D E F G H I J K L M N O P Q R S T U V W X Y Z

noisy notes are all around

Oo

one
One is the first number.

octopus
An octopus is a sea creature with eight arms.

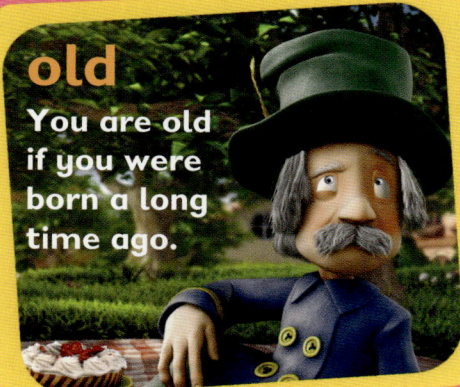

orange
An orange is a round fruit with thick peel.

old
You are old if you were born a long time ago.

owl
An owl is a bird that flies at night.

off goes the train, over the snow

Pp

palace
Zeebad lives in a large ice palace.

page
A page is part of a book.

paper
You write on paper.

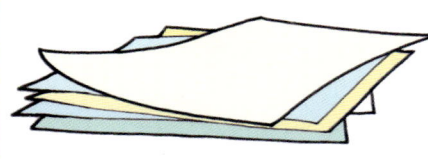

paint ✳
You paint with a brush to colour a picture.

pen
You use a pen to write or draw.

Puff! Puff! Puff! Watch it go

piano

A piano is an instrument with black and white keys.

pretty

A pretty girl has a nice looking face.

plant

A plant grows out of the ground.

pull *

You can pull with your arms.

play *

When you play you have fun.

push *

You push a wheelbarrow.

Qq

queue
You line up in a queue to wait for a bus.

queen
A queen is a woman who rules a country.

quick
You are quick when you move fast.

question
You ask a question to find out something.

'WHAT IS YOUR NAME?'

quiet
You are quiet when you make little noise. Florence is a quiet girl.

quiet Florence in a queue

Rr

rain

Rain is water falling from the sky.

rabbit

A rabbit is an animal with long ears. Dylan is a rabbit.

rainbow

Sun shines through rain to make a rainbow.

race

The friends are in a race against Zeebad to find the diamonds.

read *

You read words written in books or on signs.

rabbit jumps and runs for you

ride ✳
The friends ride on the train.

rocket
A rocket sends a spacecraft into space.

river
A river is a large stream of water.

roundabout
The Magic Roundabout goes round and round.

road
Cars and buses travel on a road.

run ✳
You move your legs quickly to run.

Ss

sing *

Ermintrude loves to sing loudly.

sad

You are sad when you feel unhappy.

small

When something is small it is not large.

scarf

Brian wears a scarf around his neck to keep warm.

snail

A snail is a small animal with a shell. Brian is a snail.

Soldier Sam makes his salute

snow

Cold snow falls on the roundabout.

sugar

Dougal loves sweet things made of sugar.

soldier

Sam is a soldier who wears a uniform and fights.

sun

It is warm and bright when the sun shines.

song

Ermintrude likes to sing songs.

sweets

The Candy Seller sells sweets made of sugar.

Tt

tall

A tall person is high off the ground.

take *

When you take something you remove it.

tap

Water comes out of a tap when you turn it on.

talk *

When you talk you speak to someone.

temple

A temple is a religious building. The friends visit a temple.

tiny train goes toot, toot, toot!

throne

A throne is a grand seat.

tree

A tree is a tall plant with leaves.

time

A watch shows the time.

trousers

Dylan wears blue trousers on his legs.

train

The train has an engine and carriages.

tunnel

The train goes through a tunnel inside the mountain.

Uu

uniform

Soldier Sam wears a uniform.

ugly

If something is ugly it is not nice to look at.

upset

Dougal is upset to see Florence trapped inside the Magic Roundabout.

umbrella

You use an umbrella to keep dry when it rains.

use *

You use a map to help you find your way.

unlucky Brian upside down

Vv

village

A village is a small collection of houses.

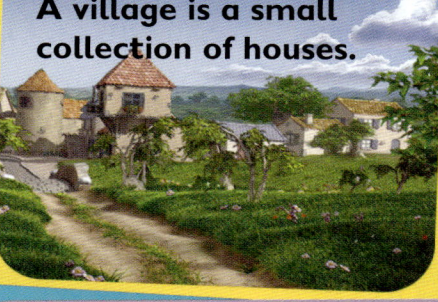

vase

You put flowers in a vase.

violin

You play a violin with a bow.

vegetable

A vegetable is a plant that you can eat.

volcano

A volcano is a mountain with a hole in the top, full of hot rock.

A B C D E F G H I J K L M N O P Q R S T U V W X Y Z

very bad Zeebad with a very big frown

Ww

water
Rivers and seas are made up of water.

walk *
You walk with your legs.

weather
Snow, rain and sunshine are types of weather.

wall
A wall is made of brick or stone.

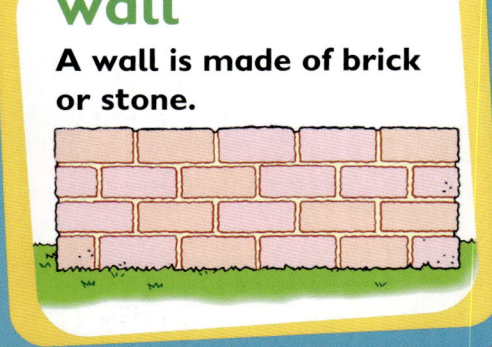

wheel
The train has wheels that turn round to make it move.

whirling wheels go round and round

wind

Wind is air moving.

wood

A wood is where a group of trees grow.

window

A window is a space in a wall to let in light.

word

You use words when you speak or write.

wizard

Zeebad is an evil wizard who does bad magic.

write *

You write words for other people to read.

A B C D E F G H I J K L M N O P Q R S T U V W X Y Z

Xx

Yy

X-ray
An X-ray shows the inside of your body.

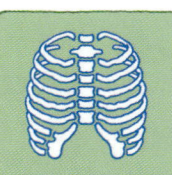

yawn
Ermintrude yawns when she is tired.

xylophone
A xylophone is a musical instrument with wooden or metal bars.

yell *
When you yell you shout loudly.

yawning Dylan lays down his head

yes
You say yes when you agree with something.

Zz

young
You are young if you were born a short time ago.

zip
You use a zip to do up some clothes.

yoghurt
You make yoghurt from sour milk.

zoo
You can see wild animals in a zoo.

Zebedee says 'Time for bed'

Friends from The Magic Roundabout™

Florence

Ermintrude

Dylan

Dougal

Zebedee

Zeebad

Soldier Sam

Brian

Train

Useful words for writing

These are words we use a lot in our writing.

a
about
adventure
after
again
all
am
an
and
another
are
as
at
away

back
ball
be
because
bed
been
big
boy
brother
but
by

call
called
came
can
can't
cat
children
come
could
couldn't
cross

dad
day
did
dig
do
dog
don't
door
down

end
every
everyone

first
for
from

get
girl
give
go
going
good
got

had
half
has
have
he
help
her
here
him
his
home
house
how

I
if
in
inside
is
it

jump
just

last
laugh
like
liked
little
live
lived
look
looked
lots
love

made
magic
make
man
many
may
me
more
much
mum
must
my

name	said	under
new	saw	up
next	school	us
night	see	
no	seen	very
not	she	
now	should	want
	sister	was
of	sit	water
off	so	way
old	some	we
on		went
once	take	were
one	than	what
or	thank	when
our	that	where
out	the	who
over	their	why
	them	will
people	then	with
play	there	would
please	these	
pull	they	yes
pulled	this	you
push	three	your
pushed	time	
put	to	
	too	
ran	took	
room	tree	
run	two	

51

Verbs

Verbs are words that describe things we do.

add 2+5=	draw
bounce	dream
call	drink
carry	eat
cry	escape
dance	fall

find	**jump**
freeze	**keep**
go	**kick**
grow	**laugh**
hear	**like**
hide	**look**

lose

make

march

mend

open

paint

play

pull

push

read

ride

run

say

see

sing

take

talk

taste

touch

use

walk

write

yawn

yell

Colours

Ermintrude loves looking at the different colours of the flowers in the garden.

white

orange

brown

blue

purple

green

yellow

red

black

pink

My body

These are the parts of your body.

head

hair

eye

nose

ear

mouth

arm

hand

elbow

leg

knee

foot

Days of the week

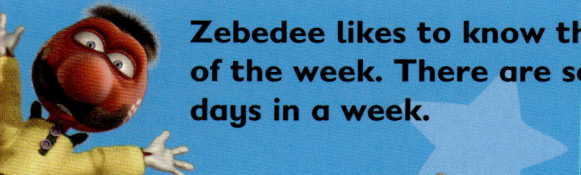

Zebedee likes to know the days of the week. There are seven days in a week.

Monday

Tuesday

Wednesday

Thursday

Friday

Saturday

Sunday

Months of the year

Brian always knows which month of the year it is. There are twelve months in a year.

January

July

February

August

March

September

April

October

May

November

June

December

59

Numbers

Dougal likes to count the number of sweets he has. The first number in this list is zero (0) and the last number is twenty (20).

zero	0	
one	1	🍬
two	2	🍬🍬
three	3	🍬🍬🍬
four	4	🍬🍬🍬🍬
five	5	🍬🍬🍬🍬🍬
six	6	🍬🍬🍬🍬🍬🍬
seven	7	🍬🍬🍬🍬🍬🍬🍬
eight	8	🍬🍬🍬🍬🍬🍬🍬🍬
nine	9	🍬🍬🍬🍬🍬🍬🍬🍬🍬

ten	10	🍬🍬🍬🍬🍬🍬🍬🍬🍬🍬
eleven	11	🍬🍬🍬🍬🍬🍬🍬🍬🍬🍬🍬
twelve	12	🍬🍬🍬🍬🍬🍬🍬🍬🍬🍬🍬🍬
thirteen	13	🍬🍬🍬🍬🍬🍬🍬🍬🍬🍬🍬🍬🍬
fourteen	14	🍬🍬🍬🍬🍬🍬🍬🍬🍬🍬🍬🍬🍬🍬
fifteen	15	🍬🍬🍬🍬🍬🍬🍬🍬🍬🍬🍬🍬🍬🍬🍬
sixteen	16	🍬🍬🍬🍬🍬🍬🍬🍬🍬🍬🍬🍬🍬🍬🍬🍬
seventeen	17	🍬🍬🍬🍬🍬🍬🍬🍬🍬🍬🍬🍬🍬🍬🍬🍬🍬
eighteen	18	🍬🍬🍬🍬🍬🍬🍬🍬🍬🍬🍬🍬🍬🍬🍬🍬🍬🍬
nineteen	19	🍬🍬🍬🍬🍬🍬🍬🍬🍬🍬🍬🍬🍬🍬🍬🍬🍬🍬🍬
twenty	20	🍬🍬🍬🍬🍬🍬🍬🍬🍬🍬🍬🍬🍬🍬🍬🍬🍬🍬🍬🍬

The alphabet

Dylan uses the letters of the alphabet to make words.

Aa

Bb

Cc

Dd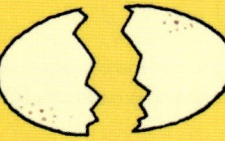

Ee

Ff

Gg

Hh

Ii

Jj

Kk

Ll

M m

N n

O o

P p

Q q

R r

S s

T t

U u

V v

W w

X x

Y y

YOGHURT

Z z